The KidHaven Science Library

Fossils

by Diane A. Kelly

KIDHAVEN PRESS
An imprint of Thomson Gale, a part of The Thomson Corporation

THOMSON
━━━━✦━━━ ™
GALE

Detroit • New York • San Francisco • San Diego • New Haven, Conn. • Waterville, Maine • London • Munich

For more information, contact
KidHaven Press
27500 Drake Rd.
Farmington Hills, MI 48331-3535
Or you can visit our Internet site at http://www.gale.com

LIBRARY OF CONGRESS CATALOGING-IN-PUBLICATION DATA

Kelly, Diane A., 1969–
  Fossils / by Diane A. Kelly.
    p. cm. — (KidHaven science library)
  Includes bibliographical references and index.
  ISBN 0-7377-2636-9 (hardcover : alk. paper)
  1. Fossils—Juvenile literature. 2. Paleontology—Juvenile literature.
I. Title. II. Series.
  QE714.5.K45 2005
  560—dc22
                                     2004029853

Contents

Life from the Past

The Earth used to be very different. Three hundred twenty million years ago, all of the continents formed a single huge landmass. The part that would become North America straddled the equator. There were no flowers and no grass anywhere on Earth. Forests of club mosses as tall as ten-story buildings supported early millipedes, spiders, scorpions, and insects, including a dragonfly with a 2-foot (60 centimeters) wingspan. The first tiny reptiles hid from predatory amphibians as long as a grown man.

Many of these animals and plants went extinct long before people could see them. But we know they existed because people have found their fossils.

Buried Treasures

Fossils are the preserved remains of once living things that are at least 10,000 years old. They come in all shapes and sizes. Fossils can be huge bones, shells the size of car tires, or whole tree trunks. They can be microscopic embryos, pollen grains, or the outlines of soft jellyfish. They can be footprints left behind by dinosaurs, or ancient worm burrows dug in the mud. They can be nests with eggs. They can even be animal dung that has turned to stone, a kind of fossil called a **coprolite**.

Most living things do not become fossils. Their bodies are eaten by other living things. After an animal dies, scavengers eat its muscle and crack open its bones. Insects chew wood from dead trees to bits. Fungi and bacteria dissolve plant and animal remains in a process called rot. If a plant or animal is going to become a fossil, it must be sealed away soon after death so it rots more slowly. Many fossils form from plant and animal remains that get buried in **sediment**. Sediment is found on the bottom of streams, lakes, and the ocean. It can be

This is the fossilized skull of an Alberto-saurus, a ferocious predator that lived 75 million years ago.

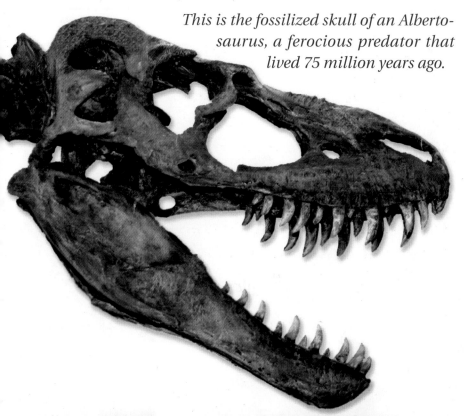

made of particles of sand, mud, or the microscopic shells of marine creatures called foraminifera.

Petrified Forest National Park in Arizona is filled with fossil trees that became fossils after getting buried in sediment. Although the area is now a desert, 200 million years ago it was a wet river valley. Forests of conifers grew on the riverbanks. When the river flooded, the water uprooted the trees and washed them downstream. Some of the logs got buried in the sand and mud at the bottom of the river. Because they were covered by sediment, these logs rotted much more slowly than usual. As the logs decayed, groundwater carrying a mineral called silica soaked through the wood. Some of the silica hardened inside of the log and turned it to stone. This process is called **lithification**. When erosion exposed the petrified wood mil-

The structure of the interior of this petrified log is perfectly intact, even after millions of years.

lions of years later, scientists found that the structure of the original wood was perfectly preserved. Even the tiny walls surrounding its cells were still visible under a microscope.

Pressed Down

Wood, shell, and bone are more likely to fossilize than soft tissues like leaves or flesh because they rot very slowly. But soft tissues can sometimes become fossils if they are buried quickly in very fine sediment. As more and more sediment collects on top of them, the soft tissues get squeezed flatter and flatter. Eventually, they turn into a thin film of carbon. If the carbon is washed away, the fossil that is left behind is called an **impression**. It is a picture of the outer surface of the fossilized plant or animal. When the sediment is very fine-grained, the fossil impression can preserve details of skin, hair, feathers, or leaves.

In the late nineteenth century, a series of extraordinary fossil skeletons were discovered in a German limestone quarry. The bones looked like they belonged to a small dinosaur called Compsognathus. Each skeleton had toothy jaws, sharp claws on its fingers and toes, and a long bony tail. But the fine-grained mud that had buried the animals also captured something surprising: Impressions of feathers surrounded the skeletons. The imprints were so detailed that the tiny zipperlike **barbules**

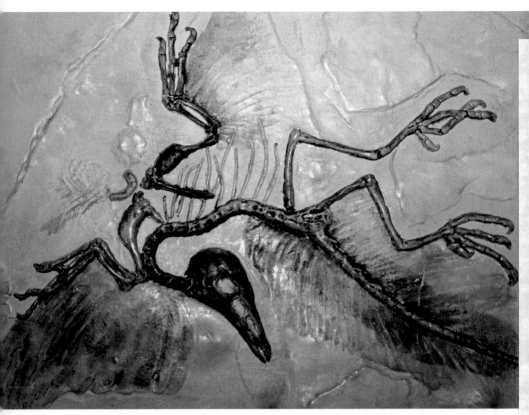

This fossil of a prehistoric bird known as Archaeopteryx is so well preserved that even its feathers can be seen.

of the feathers could be seen under a microscope. The feathers showed that these were not fossils of small dinosaurs. They were birds. Scientists named them Archaeopteryx, which means "old wing."

Frozen in Time

Impressions show what soft tissues looked like even though the original tissue is destroyed. In some very rare fossils, the soft tissues can be preserved for thousands of years.

The partial remains of mammoths and woolly rhinoceroses have been found buried in the arctic permafrost of Alaska and Siberia. The frozen ground can preserve the animals' skin and muscle for tens of thousands of years. One baby mammoth found in Siberia had been frozen for 40,000 years, but still had chestnut-brown hair on its skin and food in its stomach.

Frozen fossils are not perfect. Often parts of them have been destroyed by scavengers. And the animals

How a Fish Becomes a Fossil

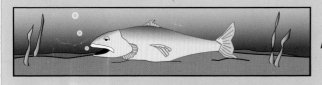

A fish dies.

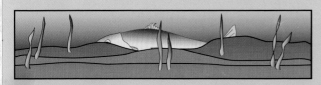

Sediment covers the fish, causing it to rot very slowly.

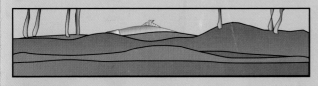

As more and more sediment builds up, it flattens the fish, leaving an impression of the animal in the soft sediment.

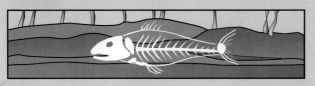

Over time, the soft parts of the fish decay, leaving the bones and the impression to harden into a rocklike fossil.

must have taken several days to freeze after they died, because their tissue usually stinks of decaying meat. Scientists who study these fossils have to work in giant refrigerators. If these fossils start to thaw, they will quickly rot away.

Perfect Preservation

There is one way to perfectly preserve soft tissues as fossils. If small animals and plants are sealed in **amber**, the amber keeps out the bacteria that would make the tissues rot. Even though the fossils are millions of years old, they look exactly the same as when the plant or animal was alive.

Amber is fossilized pine resin. It came from trees that leaked thick, sticky sap. During the day the Sun

Trapped in pine tree sap, this insect was fossilized in amber, looking exactly as it did millions of years ago.

warmed the sap until it flowed down the tree trunk. While it was warm, small plants and animals sometimes got stuck in it. If the animals were very small, they were not strong enough to get out again. The ripples from their struggles are still visible in some pieces of amber. At night, the sap cooled and hardened, trapping the animals inside. Eventually the globs of sap fell off the tree and were covered by dirt. Over millions of years, the sap slowly hardened into amber. Amber from the Baltic region of Europe is about 30 to 40 million years old. Amber from Central America is close to 120 million years old.

Fossils trapped in amber do not get crushed. This makes very delicate structures easy to see. When things like flowers and insects fossilize in rock, they get squished flat. It is sometimes hard for scientists to figure out what a flattened fossil looked like when it was alive. But fossil ants in amber are so well preserved that scientists can see microscopic details on their bodies. They can even find tiny mites and worms that were living on the ants as parasites. Amber has also preserved bees, mushrooms, feathers, and even a whole tree frog!

Fossils form in many different ways. But no matter what they look like, fossils are records of ancient living things. Scientists can use these records to learn about extinct animals, extinct plants, and how the Earth has changed over millions of years.

Great Fossil Finds

Scientists who study ancient life are called **paleontologists**. They can study fossils in museums, but the best part of their job is going out to find new fossils. Looking for fossils is exciting, but it takes hard work and a bit of luck.

Fossils are usually embedded in layers of rock made of hardened sediment. So paleontologists look for fossils in places where it is easy to see bare **sedimentary rock**. They may look in deserts or on cliffs, in road cuts or in mines. They go back to the same places over and over again because new fossils are exposed by **erosion** as wind and rain wears away the rock. Erosion exposes new fossils, but it also destroys them over time. A fossil hunter has to find a fossil after it becomes visible but before it is completely worn away.

Paleontologists have to be ready to be surprised. They never know what kind of fossil they might find when they start looking. They may walk for miles looking at the ground before spotting a tiny bit of bone or shell. With luck, more of the fossil is hidden inside the rock, ready to be chipped out and taken back to the lab. And sometimes the fossil is a great discovery that answers questions about life long ago.

New Pieces

Sometimes paleontologists find only one or two tiny pieces of an ancient **organism's** body. It can be very hard to figure out what the organism looked like or how it acted from such little fragments. Scientists have to make guesses based on the pieces they have and the facts they know about related organisms. They get the chance to check their guesses whenever someone discovers a more complete fossil.

A team of paleontologists in search of fossils chisels away at rock on a cliff face in Alberta, Canada.

In 2000 paleontologist Paul Sereno led an expedition to the Sahara desert in Africa to look for dinosaurs. On earlier trips his team had found fossils of dinosaurs that had never been seen before. But this time they found something different. They found the bones of an enormous 110-million-year-old crocodilian.

The animal was Sarcosuchus imperator. Paleontologists had found a few of its bones in the 1960s. But they could not learn much about Sarcosuchus from a few back plates and pieces of its skull. They could tell it was a big animal, but they did not have enough information to figure out how big or how heavy it had been.

Sereno's team had found the most complete Sarcosuchus skeleton that anyone had ever seen. By comparing it to the other fossils, they were able to estimate how big it was. Sarcosuchus was as long as a school bus, and probably weighed about 40 tons (18.1 kg)! It is the largest animal of its type known to have lived. It may have even eaten dinosaurs.

Changing Minds

Sometimes a fossil makes scientists think differently about an organism. The first oviraptor fossil was discovered in Mongolia in 1923. It was a weird-looking animal. Like many carnivorous dinosaurs, it ran on two legs and had arms with grasping

This is a replica of Sarcosuchus imperator, a giant crocodilian that lived in Africa 110 million years ago.

hands. But it had a heavy toothless beak instead of a mouthful of teeth. And the top of its head was covered with a frilly crest of bone.

The oviraptor's skull was found on top of a nest of eggs. The scientists on this expedition had been finding a lot of dinosaur eggs. They lay in neat circles on the desert floor—in nests. Their shells had a crinkled surface that made it easy to tell they were all laid by the same kind of animal. But the tiny bones of the baby dinosaurs inside the eggs had not survived. The team decided that the nests probably belonged to the most common dinosaur they

A display from a museum in Mongolia shows an oviraptor skeleton standing over a fossilized oviraptor egg.

found in the area, a small relative of Triceratops called Protoceratops. Because the oviraptor skull was so close to a nest, the researchers thought that the carnivorous dinosaur had died while eating Protoceratops eggs. This was how the fossil got its name. The word oviraptor means "egg thief."

Seventy years later, paleontologists Michael Novacek and Mark Norell led an expedition back to Mongolia. Their team found fossils in a new location called Ukhaa Togold. This part of the desert contained an enormous number of fossil dinosaurs, mammals, and lizards. It also had nests of fossil eggs.

The eggs looked exactly the same as the ones found in the 1920s, but these eggs were better preserved. Tiny fossilized bones of embryonic dinosaurs were inside the eggs. But to the scientists' surprise they were not Protoceratops babies. They were baby oviraptors!

The team also found another adult oviraptor on top of a nest of eggs. This fossil was not just lying over the eggs. It was sitting on top of the nest. With this new evidence, scientists changed their mind

This oviraptor died while protecting her nest containing more than twenty eggs in Mongolia's Gobi Desert.

about oviraptor. They realized that the "egg thief" was actually a good parent.

Solving Mysteries

Sometimes a new fossil can solve mysteries about ancient living things. For many years, paleontologists wanted to know when humanlike apes called **hominids** started to walk on two legs. Modern humans walk on two legs. Chimpanzees and gorillas, the closest living relatives of humans, knuckle-walk using all four legs. But the hominid fossils paleontologists had to study at the time were very young—less than 3 million years old. They did not tell scientists whether **bipedal** walking had evolved early or late in hominids.

Then, in 1978, paleontologist Mary Leakey found fossilized hominid footprints at a site in Laetoli, Tanzania. When some of her friends had come to visit her field site, Leakey showed them the places her team had found fossils. As they walked back to camp, her friends began to throw dried elephant dung at each other. When one of them ducked out of the way, he fell down and noticed what appeared to be footprints in the rock.

When Leakey's team excavated the site, they found thousands of tracks in an ancient ash bed. It had formed when rain fell on newly settled volcanic

Mary Leakey studies hominid footprints fossilized in a bed of volcanic ash in Tanzania, Africa.

ash. Like wet cement, the wet ash captured the footprints of the animals that walked over it. It preserved footprints from insects and hares, birds, rhinos, and elephants. And it preserved an 80-foot-(27 meter)-long series of hominid footprints.

Fossil footprints are one kind of **trace fossil**. They are fossilized behavior. They do not show much of what an animal's body looked like. Instead, they are clues that show how an animal acted. The Laetoli trackway contained two sets of hominid footprints. They may have been walking together. One set of footprints was larger than the other. And the footprints looked like the prints a barefoot person would leave in sand. There were no handprints or traces of knuckle-walking in the hardened ash. These were tracks of bipedal animals.

When the ash was dated, the scientists found it was about 3.6 million years old. The tracks were a million years older than any fossil hominid bones found at that time. They showed that walking on two legs is a very old trait for hominids.

New discoveries like these often change the way scientists think about ancient living things. The cycle of discovery and changing ideas never ends.

Understanding Fossils

Fossils can be hard to figure out. They can be squashed flat or twisted in the rock so they no longer look the way they did when they were alive. They can get broken into pieces that have to be put back together. Sometimes a fossil is only one part of an animal or plant. It might be part of an arm, or part of the mouth, or some leaves, or the roots. The rest of the organism might have been eaten or rotted away before it was buried. Paleontologists have to use tools to help them make sense of the fossils they study.

Looking Hard

The most important tools that paleontologists use are their eyes. They look at a new fossil carefully and compare it to other fossils and to living animals or plants. They look for features that are unique to the fossil and features that it shares with other organisms. Researchers may study fossils

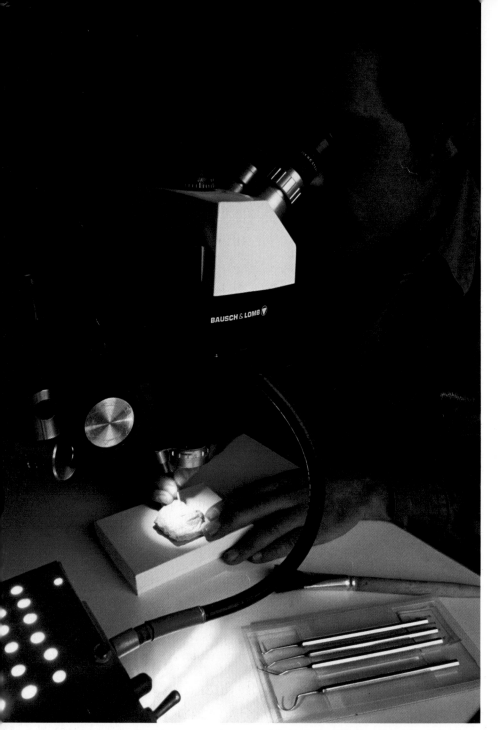

A paleontologist studies the fine details of a fossil under a high-powered microscope.

under a microscope to see parts that are invisible to the naked eye. They may even put the fossil under water to make the bumps and ridges on its surface easier to see.

Looking at a fossil helps scientists figure out what the animal was like when it was alive. It is like putting a puzzle together when some of the pieces are missing. Sometimes it takes a long time. One ancient animal, Anomalocaris, was first found in many pieces. Scientists had pieces from most of the animal. But they had never seen anything like it before, and all of its close relatives were extinct. At first, researchers thought each piece of Anomalocaris was a different animal. They thought its mouth was a jellyfish, and one of its claws was part of a shrimp. It took almost a hundred years before a complete Anomalocaris fossil was found. When paleontologists looked at the new fossil, they realized that the pieces were not different animals, but were all part of a single predator unlike any animal alive today.

An Inside Look

Every part of a fossil tells a story about how that organism lived. The more paleontologists can see of a fossil, the more they can learn about it. Until recently, scientists could see a fossil only after they completely removed the rock that surrounded it. There was no easy way to look inside it. The only way to see inside a fossil was to slowly destroy it by chipping away its outside. But new technology now lets scientists see inside fossils without damaging them.

In 1967 the National Geographic Society was given an intact elephant bird egg. Elephant birds were flightless birds related to ostriches and emus. They lived in forests on the African island of Madagascar until the seventeenth century. They were huge—taller than a grown man and as heavy as a small car. They also laid the biggest eggs anyone has ever seen. An elephant bird egg could hold 2 gallons (8 liters) of water. But eggshells are fragile. Most elephant bird eggs are found in pieces. Unbroken eggs are very rare.

Medical X-rays showed paleontologists there was something inside the egg, but the picture was too blurry to make out many details. They could only see a few bones sticking out of a jumbled mass at one end of the egg. The scientists wanted to learn which bones had fossilized and which had rotted away, but could not find out without destroying the eggshell. So they waited. Thirty years later, they finally had their chance to find out.

In 1999 researchers sent the elephant bird egg to the University of Texas, Austin, to be photographed by a powerful digital X-ray camera. This camera can take photographs of the inside of a fossil. It uses X-rays that are much more powerful than the X-rays doctors use. Stronger X-rays produce more detailed photographs, but they also kill living tissue. Fortunately, the X-rays cannot hurt fossils because they are already dead.

A tribesman in Madagascar holds a fossilized egg of an elephant bird, an extinct bird related to ostriches and emus.

Instead of slicing the real egg into pieces, the camera took a series of pictures from one end of the egg to the other. Each picture showed one thin slice of the egg. Researchers used a computer to assemble the photographs into a three-dimensional picture of the egg's inside. The result was amazing. The old X-ray pictures had showed a few blurry bones. The new pictures showed that more than half of the bones of a baby elephant bird were in the egg. Pictures of each bone could be separated in the computer for study. The scientists were even able to make models of each bone and build a small replica of the fossil embryo's skull.

Making Models

Paleontologists want to learn what fossil organisms looked like inside and out. They also want to understand how the organisms lived. They look carefully at fossils to try to understand how ancient plants grew and how ancient animals ate and moved. A fossil can give them many ideas. But it may not help them test their ideas, because the fossil can no longer grow, or eat, or walk. Using models can help. Researchers can build mechanical models to test how hard a fossil animal could bite. They can make animated computer models to test ideas about how it moved. Or they may compare a fossil to closely related living **species**. The living organism becomes a model for the fossil's behavior. Combining data from fossils and models gives scientists more information about an ancient organism's life.

Models helped biologist Stephen Gatesy understand a very strange set of fossil footprints from Greenland. All of the tracks were made by the same animal, a human-sized carnivorous dinosaur. Some of the tracks were shallow three-toed footprints with impressions of foot pads, claws, and skin. But other tracks looked like they had been squished and folded. Their toe marks looked like long, deep channels in the rock. And they had four toes instead of three. But why were these tracks so weird?

Gatesy thought that the weird footprints might have been made when the dinosaurs walked through deep mud. In dinosaurs with four toes, one toe was small and close to the ankle. It would not have touched the ground when the dinosaur walked on hard dirt. But what if the animal had sunk down into the mud? If its foot went deep enough, the little toe might have left a mark. He tested his idea by getting

Scientists use digital X-rays to see inside fossilized elephant bird eggs (shown).

How Paleontologists Figure Out a Fossil's Age

If a fossil is less than about 50,000 years old, scientists can determine the fossil's age by measuring how much Carbon-14 it contains.

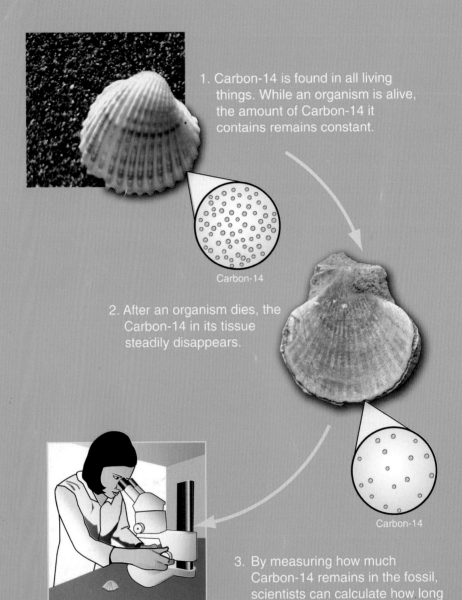

1. Carbon-14 is found in all living things. While an organism is alive, the amount of Carbon-14 it contains remains constant.

Carbon-14

2. After an organism dies, the Carbon-14 in its tissue steadily disappears.

Carbon-14

3. By measuring how much Carbon-14 remains in the fossil, scientists can calculate how long ago it died.

turkeys and guinea fowl to walk through a mix of wet sand and clay. Ground birds and carnivorous dinosaurs are both bipedal. They also have similar feet. Gatesy used the birds to model for dinosaurs walking.

Gatesy found that when the birds walked over damp soil, they left footprints that looked like the three-toed dinosaur footprints. But when they walked in wet mud their feet sank deep into the soil and left footprints like the strange folded tracks. The folds appeared because the birds pulled their toes

Paleontologists use models of fossilized organisms to learn more about how ancient animals lived.

together when they lifted their foot out of the mud. The experiment showed the fossil tracks changed shape because the dinosaur had walked in some gooey mud.

Paleontologists do a lot more than dig up bones. They study fossils with tools that teach them different things. When they combine all the things they have learned, they know more about how an ancient organism looked and acted.

Fossils Are Clues

A fossil teaches paleontologists about a particular ancient organism. It is also a clue to the world of the past. Paleontologists act like detectives. They look at many fossils and the places they are found to gather clues. Then they piece together answers to questions about how living things and the Earth have changed over time.

Changing Life

Fossils show that living things have evolved, or changed over time. Each fossil is a snapshot of a living thing at a particular time. By looking at fossils from different times, scientists can trace changes between an ancestor and its descendants.

Whales and dolphins are mammals. But they do not look much like mammals that live on land. They are shaped like fish. They have no hind legs and swim by beating their tail up and down. Their nose is found on the top of their head. Scientists can tell **cetaceans** are mammals because they have some traits that are found only in mammals. They make milk for their babies. And some cetaceans even have whiskers, although most are hairless. But if whales and dolphins are mammals like cows and hippos, how did they lose their back legs?

Paleontologists have learned how whales lost their hind legs by studying fossil cetaceans from different points in Earth's history. Scientists can tell the fossils are all cetaceans because they share an S-shaped anchor on the bones surrounding their ears. This anchor is found only in cetaceans. Without this clue, paleontologists would not have guessed that the earliest known cetacean was related to whales. Pakicetus did not look like a whale at all. It was a wolf-sized land animal that lived about 52 million years ago. It had front and hind legs and could run.

Over millions of years, cetacean hind limbs got smaller and smaller. Ambulocetus was an alligator-sized cetacean that lived 49 million years ago. It had four short legs, but it was better at swimming than at walking. Ambulocetus was an amphibious predator, spending time on both land and in the water. It probably hunted by hiding underwater in small rivers and ambushing animals that came to drink.

Three million years later a cetacean called Rodhocetus had short legs with long feet like a seal's flippers. It may have been able to drag itself onto the beach with its stubby legs, but it probably spent most of its time swimming in deep water off the coast.

Forty-three million years ago, the now-extinct whale Basilosaurus could be found in oceans all

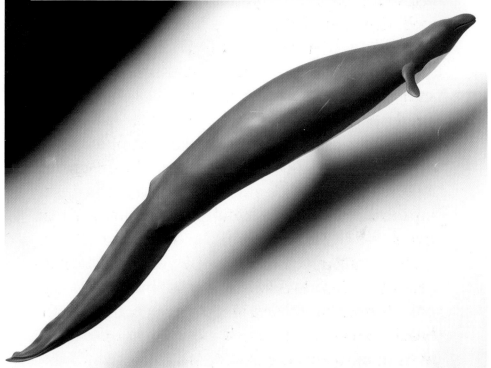

Fossils of the now-extinct Basilosaurus (top) showed how the 60-foot-long whale (bottom) evolved over time.

over the world. It was 60 feet (18 meters) long—far too big to ever get out of the water. But it still had a pair of tiny hind legs, complete with knees and toes. Its legs were too small to swim with. Basilosaurus swam with its long flexible body. Modern whales and dolphins are descended from animals like Basilosaurus.

Moving Mountains

Fossils also show that the Earth has changed over time. The continents are part of huge plates of rock that move very slowly around the surface of the Earth. As the plates move, continents can split apart and new oceans form in between them. The plates can also crash together and form mountains. This process is called **plate tectonics**. It happens too slowly for people to see. But fossils give scientists clues that it happens.

The top of Mount Everest is the last place any-one might expect to see a seashell. But fossils of marine animals like clamlike **brachiopods** and sea lilies are found in the mountain rock. This tells scientists that the mountains were once the bottom of an ocean. Over millions of years, India has pushed north into Asia like a giant bulldozer. The rock that was on the bottom of the ocean between the two continents was pushed up in folds to form the Himalayan mountains.

Fossils show that some continents were once connected. A fossil fern called Glossopteris is found in rocks in South America, Africa, India, and Australia. These places are separated by very large oceans. Ferns must be near freshwater and soil to reproduce. They cannot float or fly across the ocean. But if the continents were once part of one huge supercontinent, the ferns could have spread over the land. Their fossils were separated later as the continents moved apart. Glossopteris went extinct about 206 million years ago. This is a clue that tells scientists South America, Africa, India, and Australia were parts of a single supercontinent

This sea lily fossil found on Mount Everest proves that the Himalayas were once the bottom of an ocean.

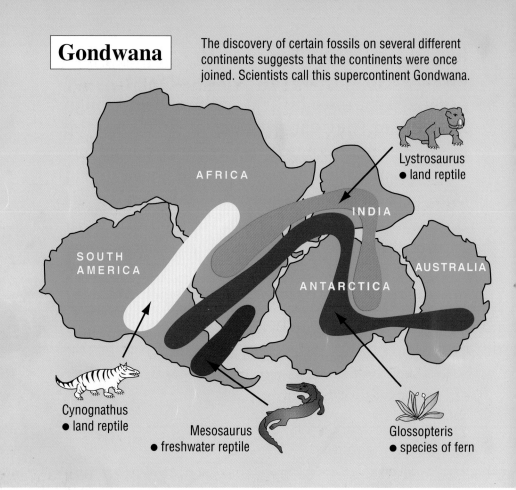

Gondwana

The discovery of certain fossils on several different continents suggests that the continents were once joined. Scientists call this supercontinent Gondwana.

AFRICA

INDIA

SOUTH AMERICA

ANTARCTICA

AUSTRALIA

Lystrosaurus
● land reptile

Cynognathus
● land reptile

Mesosaurus
● freshwater reptile

Glossopteris
● species of fern

Source: U.S. Geological Survey.

at least 206 million years ago. Scientists call the giant continent Gondwana.

Disappearing Act

Many of the plants and animals that once lived on these ancient continents have gone extinct. Some of them were unlike anything that is alive today. Glyptodonts were heavily armored mammals related to armadillos that were as big as a small car.

Pterosaurs were reptiles that flew on thin wings made of skin. Opabinia was a strange little **invertebrate** with five eyes and a long flexible mouth. None of these animals have modern descendants. People only know they existed because of their fossils.

Fossils also show that many species sometimes go extinct in a short period of time. This is called a **mass extinction**. A mass extinction affects organisms all over the world, both on the land and in the ocean. Large and small organisms die out. Even tiny plankton species go extinct. Paleontologists identify a mass extinction when the fossils of many unrelated organisms disappear from the rock layers at the same time. Fossils that were common in older layers of rock suddenly vanish.

This pterosaur fossil shows the reptile's thin wings and very long jaws.

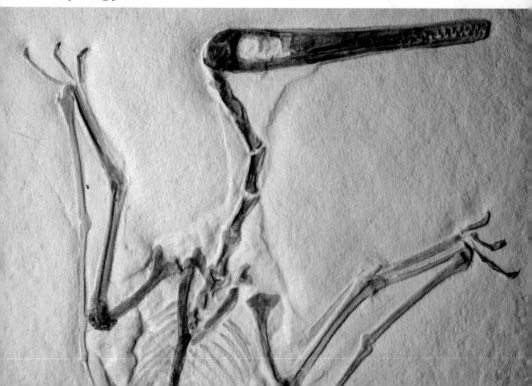

Paleontologists have found evidence for six large mass extinctions over the past 550 million years. Many scientists think they were caused when small asteroids hit the Earth. The most famous one happened 65 million years ago. Eighty-five percent of all living species died, including all of the dinosaurs, pterosaurs, and marine reptiles. Ammonites, shelled relatives of squid that could grow as large as car tires, also went extinct. But the largest mass extinction happened 245 million years ago. As many as 96 percent of all marine species died. So did more than three-quarters of the land species.

In this drawing, a Tyrannosaurus rex watches a huge asteroid slam into the Earth. The impact wiped out all of the world's dinosaur species.

The victims included shelled **arthropods** called trilobites and a group of heavily armored fish called placoderms.

Every time there is a mass extinction, new species evolve from the organisms that survive. Small reptiles that survived the largest extinction gave rise to dinosaurs and mammals. When the dinosaurs died out, mammals and birds survived and became the dominant land animals.

Fossils tell a story about Earth's past. They are a record that let people learn how living things and the Earth itself have changed over time. And anyone can go out and find them.

amber: Fossilized pine resin.

arthropods: A group of animals that have tough external skeletons with jointed legs.

barbules: Branching segments of a feather. Barbules lock together to keep the feather smooth.

bipedal: Walking on two legs.

brachiopods: Marine animals with clamlike shells.

cetaceans: Groups of mammals that include whales and dolphins.

coprolite: Fossilized animal dung.

erosion: The process by which wind or water wears away rock.

hominids: Humanlike apes.

impression: A type of fossil formed when an organism is pressed into fine sediment. It preserves the outer surface of the fossilized plant or animal.

invertebrate: An animal that does not have a hard internal skeleton.

lithification: The process by which minerals enter formerly living materials and turn them to stone.

mass extinction: The sudden worldwide extinction of many different types of organisms.

organism: A living thing.

paleontologists: Scientists who use fossils to study ancient living things.

plate tectonics: The movement of rocky continental plates over the surface of the Earth.

sediment: Tiny particles of sand, mud, or other material that settles to the bottom of a body of water.

sedimentary rock: Rock formed from hardened layers of sediment.

species: Any one kind of organism.

trace fossil: A fossil that preserves traces of animal activity.

Books

Hannah Bonner, *When Bugs Were Big, Plants Were Strange, and Tetrapods Stalked the Earth: A Cartoon Prehistory of Life Before Dinosaurs*. Washington, DC: National Geographic Society, 2003. Describes life at the end of the Paleozoic period, before dinosaurs or mammals appeared on Earth.

Niles Eldredge, Douglas Eldredge, and Gregory Eldredge, *The Fossil Factory: A Kid's Guide to Digging Up Dinosaurs, Exploring Evolution, and Finding Fossils*. Boulder, CO: Roberts Reinhart, 2002. A fact-filled book about geology and paleontology. Includes tips for collecting fossils.

Mark Norell and Lowell Dingus, *A Nest of Dinosaurs: The Story of Oviraptor*. New York: Doubleday, 1999. Describes expeditions to the Flaming Cliffs of Mongolia and the discovery of the new oviraptor fossils.

Christopher Sloan, *Supercroc and the Origin of Crocodiles*. Washington, DC: National Geographic Society, 2002. Describes the evolution of crocodiles, including giants like Sarcosuchus.

Web Sites

The American Museum of Natural History, New York City (www.amnh.org). AMNH has the nesting oviraptor and fossil eggs on display, along with many other samples from their important fossil collection.

Digital Morphology (www.digimorph.org). The University of Texas, Austin, hosts this site. It is a public library of the images researchers there have collected from their digital X-ray camera. These include images from both fossils and living animals (and the elephant bird egg described in this book).

Leakey Foundation (www.leakeyfoundation.org). This organization focuses on research related to human origins. Its Web site includes an interactive time line describing the discovery of hominid fossils.

Museum of Paleontology at the University of California, Berkeley (www.ucmp.berkeley.edu). The MPUC hosts an online museum that includes a great introduction to fossils and what scientists can learn from them.

The National Museum of Natural History, Washington, DC (www.mnh.si.edu). NMNH is part of the Smithsonian. Its fossil halls include displays of Anomalocaris and other ancient animals.

Petrified Forest National Park, Arizona (www. nps.gov/pefo). This park has one of the world's largest concentrations of petrified wood.

Project Exploration (www.projectexploration.org). A nonprofit organization founded by paleontologist Paul Sereno and educator Gabrielle Lyon to involve the public in paleontological discoveries. Includes descriptions of Dr. Sereno's expeditions and a great list of resources.

United States Geological Survey Learning Web (www.usgs.gov/education). The USGS education page has pointers to all kinds of geology information, including fossils.

Index

mammoths, 9
mass extinction, 36–39
medical X-rays, 24
models, 26–27, 29–30
Mongolia, 14–16
Mount Everest, 34

National Geographic
    Society, 24
Norell, Mark, 16
North America, 4
Novacek, Michael, 16

Opabinia, 37
oviraptors, 14–18

Pakicetus, 32
paleontologists, 12, 21,
    23, 31
Petrified Forest National
    Park, 6–7
pine resin, 10–11
placoderms, 39
plate tectonics, 34–36
preservation, 9–11

pterosaurs, 37

Rodhocetus, 32
rot, process of, 5

Sarcosuchus imperator,
    14
sediment, 5–6, 7, 12
Sereno, Paul, 14
silica, 6

Tanzania, 18, 20
technology, 23–24,
    26–27, 29–30
tissues, soft, 7–8
trace fossils, 20, 27,
    29–30
trilobites, 39

Ukhaa Togold
    (Mongolia), 16

whales, 31–32, 34

X-rays, 24, 26

Picture Credits

Cover: © Louie Psihoyos/ CORBIS
© Daniel Aguilar/Reuters/CORBIS, 29
C. Butler / Photo Researchers, Inc., 38
© Albert Copley/Visuals Unlimited, 33 (top)
Corel, 6
© DK Limited/CORBIS, 27, 33 (bottom)
© Chris Hellier/CORBIS, 25
© Layne Kennedy/CORBIS, 22
Edward Kinsman / Photo Researchers, Inc., 10
© Sally A. Morgan; Ecoscene/CORBIS, 8
Brandy Noon, 9, 28, 36
© Louie Psihoyos/CORBIS, 13, 16, 17
John Reader/Photo Researchers, Inc., 19
© Reuters/CORBIS, 15
© Kevin Schafer/CORBIS, 37
Kaj R. Svensson / Photo Researchers, Inc., 35
© Michael S. Yamashita/CORBIS, 5

Diane A. Kelly is a biologist who has helped collect hadrosaurs in Canada, mastodons in New York, and ancient invertebrates in Illinois. She lives near a set of dinosaur tracks in western Massachusetts.